1

Where were they standing when the artist drew this picture? You can solve the puzzle by finding the missing words from the list. Use each word once only. Write the answers in the blanks.

left	between	man	Miss Small
right	two	Mr Wills	ladies

1 Miss Lucas was standing .... Mr Thomas and Miss Sands.

2 Mr Banks was standing on the left of ....

3 Mr Wills was standing on the .... of Miss Lake.

4 There were two .... between Mr Thomas and Mr Wills.

5 Miss Sands was standing on the left of ....

6 Miss Small was standing on the .... of Mr Banks.

7 There was a .... between Miss Small and Miss Lake.

8 There were .... people between Mr Thomas and Mr Banks.

2

What do they do? Can you find the missing words from the list on the right?

1 An artist often
2 A carpenter often
3 A baby often
4 A pilot often
5 A gardener often
6 Soldiers sometimes
7 A tailor sometimes
8 Authors often
9 Dentists sometimes
10 A footballer often
11 Athletes sometimes
12 Priests sometimes
13 Students sometimes
14 Surgeons sometimes
15 Hairdressers sometimes

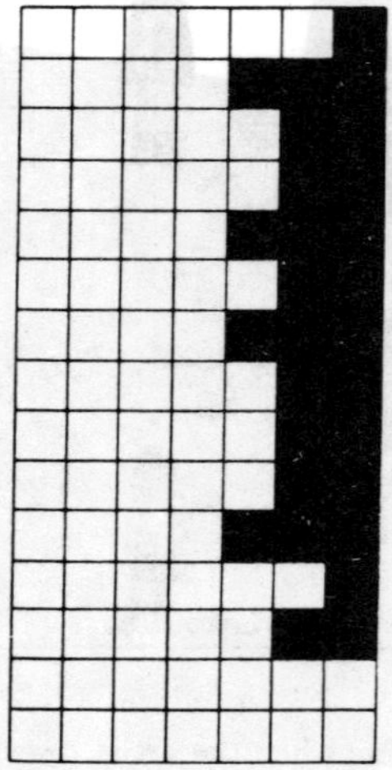

flies
write
paints
cries
saws
shampoo
preach
shoot
learn
sews
drill
kicks
jump
digs
operate

3

1 It has four legs but it cannot walk. It has a head, but it cannot see or speak. It has a foot, but it cannot kick.

What is it? ....

2 What goes up when the rain comes down? ....

4

Mr Lee | Miss Lake | Mr Davies | Mrs Jones | Mr Black | Tom

Miss Green | Mr Cole | Miss Mack | Mrs Wood | Mr Ash | Mary

What were they doing when the artist drew these pictures? Choose your verbs from this list?

riding	smiling	laughing	swimming
shaving	dancing	singing	digging
diving	jumping	running	hitting

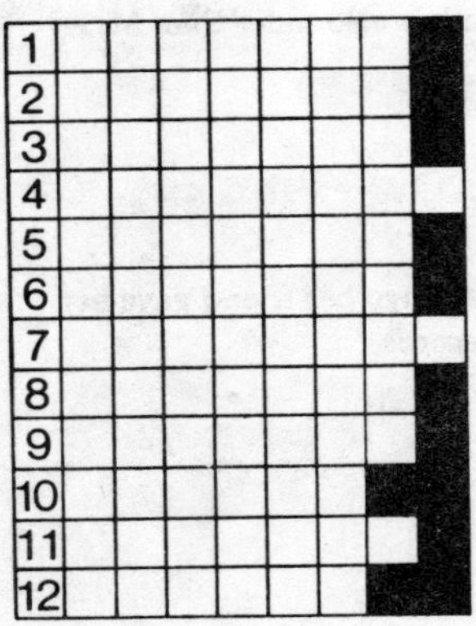

1 Mr Lee was . . .
2 Miss Lake was . . .
3 Mr Davies was . . .
4 Mrs Jones was . . .
5 Mr Black was . . .
6 Tom was . . .
7 Miss Green was . . .
8 Mr Cole was . . .
9 Miss Mack was . . .
10 Mrs Wood was . . .
11 Mr Ash was . . .
12 Mary was . . .

5

If you solve this puzzle correctly, you will need these words:

bricks	steel	leather	rubber	grass	flour
paper	wood	cotton	sugar	wool	glass

1 Walls are often made of
2 Shirts are often made of
3 Books are made of
4 Tyres are usually made of
5 Bottles are usually made of
6 Bread is made of
7 Scissors are made of
8 Desks are usually made of
9 Pullovers are often made of
10 Lawns are made of
11 Shoes are often made of
12 Sweets are made of

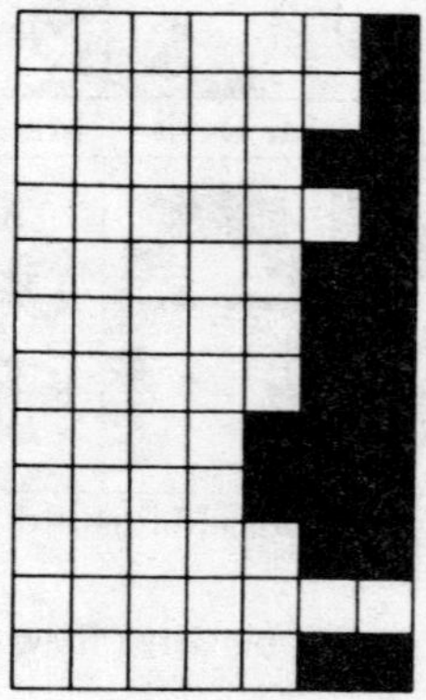

6

1 Mr Brown is taller than Mr White, and Mr Pink is also taller than Mr White.

Which of the three men is the shortest? ....

2 Miss Cox had 22 records a week ago. Three days ago her friend gave her four more. Since then she has lost one of her records.

How many has she now? ....

7

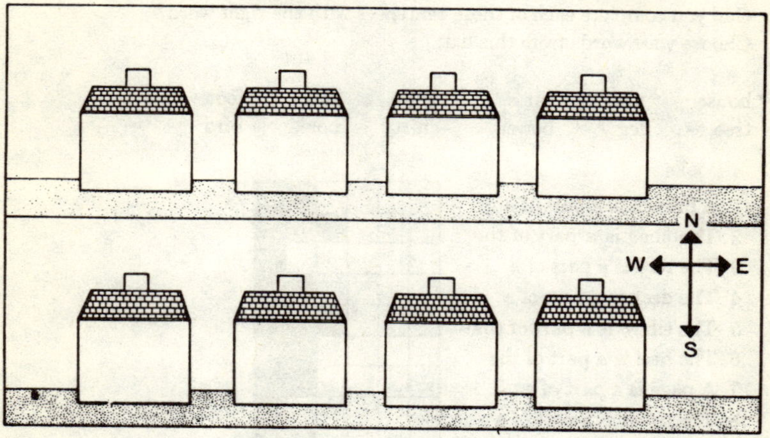

There are only eight houses in this street. Mr Grey lives on the north side of the street. He lives next to Mr Pink. Mr Pink is therefore Mr Grey's neighbour, and Mr Grey is Mr Pink's neighbour. Mr Pink's other neighbour is Mr Brown. Mr Brown's house is on the left of Mr Pink's. The other house on the north side belongs to Mr White. Mr White lives to the left of Mr Brown.

On the opposite side of the street there are four more houses. Mr Butcher lives between Mr Baker and Mr Miller. Mr Cook lives on the left of Mr Baker. Mr Miller lives opposite Mr White.

Can you write the names of the men on their houses?

8

Mr Grey and Mr Butcher have decided to change houses. Mr Grey is going to live in Mr Butcher's house, and Mr Butcher is going to live in Mr Grey's house. When they have changed houses, who will be Mr Baker's neighbour on his left?

. . . .

9

Can you complete each of these sentences with the right word?
Choose your words from this list:

house	arm	car	knife	ship	foot
tree	leg	flower	shirt	book	bird

1 A branch is a part of a
2 The knee is a part of the
3 The roof is a part of a
4 The deck is a part of a
5 The elbow is a part of the
6 The heel is a part of the
7 A page is a part of a
8 The collar is a part of a
9 A wing is a part of a
10 The handle is a part of a
11 A petal is a part of a
12 The engine is a part of a

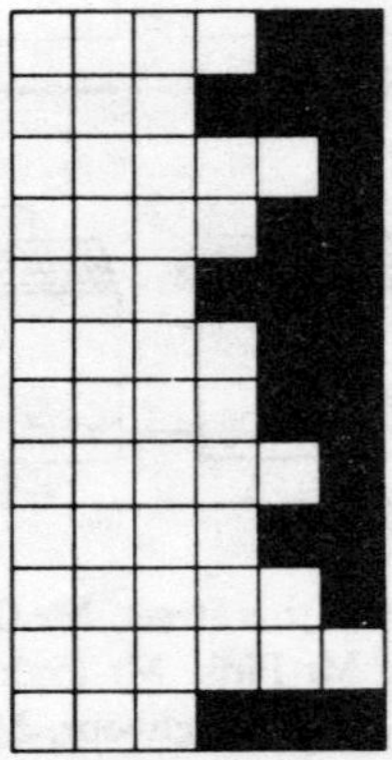

10

1 Anne is younger than her sister Karen, but she is older than her brother Steven.

Which of the three is the oldest? . . . .

2 Richard has 80 pence. A few minutes ago Bob had half this amount, but he has just given three-quarters of it to Wayne. Wayne now has as much as Richard has.

How much did Wayne have before? . . . .

11

Try to solve the puzzle below with the help of the clues and these definitions:

Artist: a person who paints pictures.
Butcher: a person who sells meat.
Chemist: a person who sells medicines.
Dentist: a person who looks after your teeth.
Grocer: a person who sells food.
Jockey: a person who rides race horses.
Joiner: a workman who makes the inside woodwork of a building.
Nurse: a person who looks after patients in hospital.
Porter: a workman who carries things.
Sailor: a man who works on a ship.

1 He sells bacon and sugar.
2 He carries your bag.
3 He sometimes rides the winner.
4 He sells pills and ointment.
5 He goes to sea.
6 He or she paints your portrait.
7 You can buy beef and mutton from him.
8 He makes cupboards and shelves.
9 She looks after sick people.
10 He sometimes fills teeth.

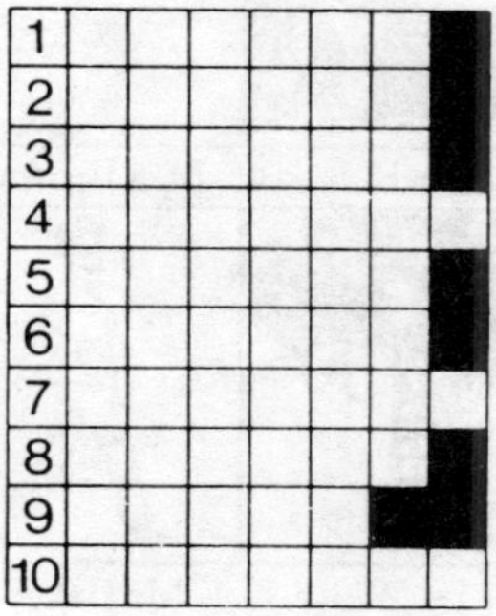

12

You can solve this puzzle by finding the missing word in each sentence. The things in the pictures all happened yesterday.

Miss James, Mr Cook, Tony, Linda, Mr Smith

Mr Ball, Mrs Brown, Mrs White, Mr Baker

1 Miss James didn't play cards yesterday; she played . . .
2 Mr Cook didn't play tennis yesterday; he played . . .
3 Tony didn't ride his pony; he rode his . . .
4 Linda didn't ride her bicycle; she rode her . . .
5 Mr Smith didn't cut his lawn; he cut his . . .
6 Mr Ball didn't cut his hedge; he cut his . . .
7 Mrs Brown didn't pick apples; she picked . . .
8 Mrs White didn't pick pears; she picked . . .
9 Mr Baker didn't go for a swim; he went for a . . .

13

This list of words will help you solve the puzzle. Use each word once only.

under	mother	mouse	cheap	kitten
uncle	brother	house	dearer	butter

1 A female parent.
2 Son of the same parents.
3 A baby cat.
4 The opposite of *above*.
5 Mr Grey lives in one.
6 The singular of 'mice'.
7 Not dear.
8 It is made from cream.
9 Not as cheap as.
10 The brother of your mother or your father.

14

There are four cars in the car park. The red car is four metres long. The blue one is ten centimetres shorter than the red one. The black one is 20 cm longer than the blue one, and the green is 15 cm shorter than the black one.

Which of the four cars is the longest? . . . .

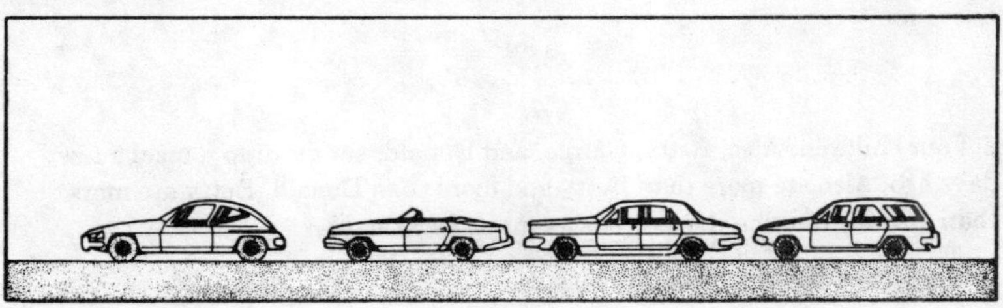

15

Can you solve this puzzle with the help of the words below? Beware! There are two more words than you need.

well	fast	little	most	asleep	closed
thin	wet	happy	dark	weak	wide

1 Large means the opposite of . . . .

2 A light colour is the opposite of a . . . . one.

3 A . . . . person is the opposite of a sad one.

4 A dry towel is the opposite of a . . . . one.

5 . . . . is the opposite of *awake*.

6 A narrow road is the opposite of a . . . . one.

7 Strong means the opposite of . . . .

8 . . . . is the opposite of *least*.

9 A man who is ill is the opposite of one who is . . . .

10 A . . . . door is the opposite of an open one.

16

1 Miss Robinson was watching television from eight o'clock till quarter past nine last night. While she was watching, it began to snow. An hour and a half later her telephone rang. Did the telephone ring while she was watching television?

. . . .

2 Four children, Alec, Betty, Carole, and Donald, sat down to a meal a few days ago. Alec ate more than Betty and more than Donald. Betty ate more than Carole, but she did not eat as much as Donald.

Which of the four children ate least? . . . .

17

Because this is the first glidogram, I have given you a list of words. You can solve the puzzle with these words:

dusty	sixth	class	basin	usual
chest	Asian		chase	scrub

1	S				
2		S			
3			S		
4				S	
5					S
6				S	
7			S		
8		S			
9	S				

1 The next after the fifth.
2 Normal; common.
3 A round open dish.
4 The top front part of the body.
5 A group of the same kind.
6 To run after and capture.
7 With dust all over it.
8 A person from Asia.
9 To clean with a wet brush.

18

1 It is yellow and round. The earth goes round it. It gives us light and warmth.

What is it? ....

2 It has four legs, but it cannot walk. It has two arms, but it cannot carry anything. It has a back, but it cannot bend.

What is it? ....

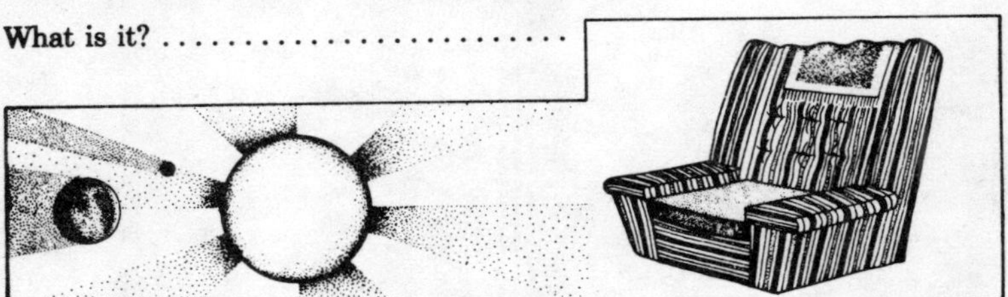

19

Can you solve this glidogram with the help of these clues?

1	G				
2		L			
3			I		
4				D	
5					O
6				G	
7			R		
8		A			
9	M				

Clues

1 A colour.
2 You put your food on this.
3 Boy or girl.
4 The buying and selling of goods.
5 A greeting.
6 The opposite of *small*.
7 The opposite of *late*.
8 He makes bread.
9 Pounds, dollars, francs.

More Clues

1 Grass is this colour.
2 The word ends with the past tense of 'to eat'.
3 The plural is *children*.
4 Importing and exporting is one kind of this.
5 You say this when you meet someone.
6 The middle letter is R.
7 The . . . bird catches the worm.
8. The first letter is B.
9. You spend it when you buy something.

20

What must they be? Find the word that is missing in each sentence and write it in the puzzle. Check your spelling with the list on the left below.

wrong
dirty
light
alive
quick
deep
female
narrow
absent
easy

1 If your hands are not clean, they must be . . . .
2 If the puzzle is not difficult, it must be . . . .
3 If the answer is not right, it must be . . . .
4 If it is not dark, it must be . . . .
5 If the water is not shallow, it must be . . . .
6 If an animal is not dead, it must be . . . .
7 If a student is not present, he must be . . . .
8 If people are not male, they must be . . . .
9 If the road is not a wide one, it must be a . . . .
10 If he is not a slow worker, he must be a . . . one.

21

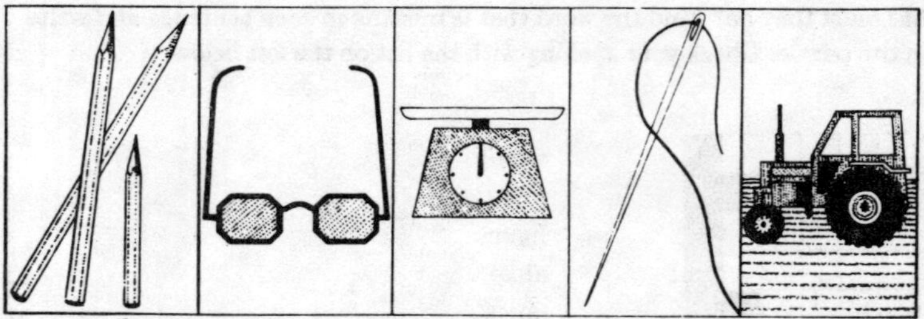

pencils | glasses | scales | a needle | a tractor

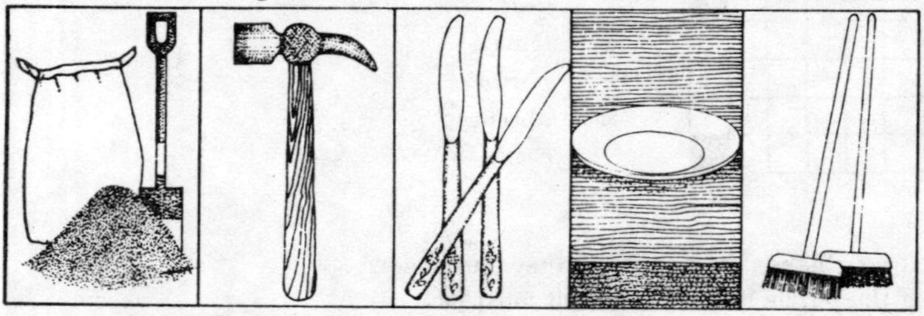

cement | a hammer | knives | a saucer | brooms

What do you do with the things in the pictures?
If you know, you can solve this puzzle.

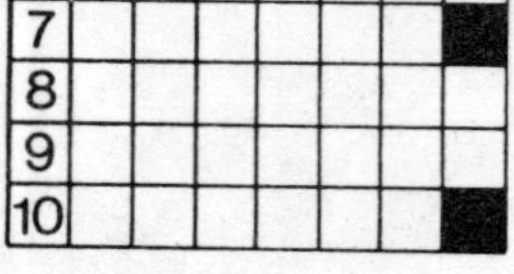

1 You sew with this.
2 You can hit nails with this.
3 You put your cup in this.
4 You cut food with these.
5 Floors are swept with these.
6 You can pull things with this.
7 Concrete is made with this.
8 You can draw with these.
9 You can see things through these.
10 Things are weighed on these.

22

You can solve this puzzle by doing what John did. He wrote R in the middle square. In the bottom square he wrote H. He put I just below R. Between H and I he wrote C. He only wrote one T, and he put that one just under the S which he wrote between O and T. In this way he spelt the name of a bird which can move very fast.

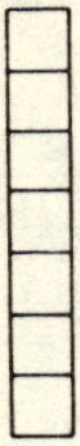

23

Can you solve this puzzle by finding eight words that end in *art*? Check your answers against this list:

tart	depart	smart	heart
dart	start	cart	part

1 To begin.
2 Some, but not all of a thing.
3 A fruit pie.
4 It is pulled by a horse.
5 Clean and well dressed.
6 You throw it at a target.
7 To leave.
8 It pumps your blood.

24

Mr Broom's horse refused the first fence.

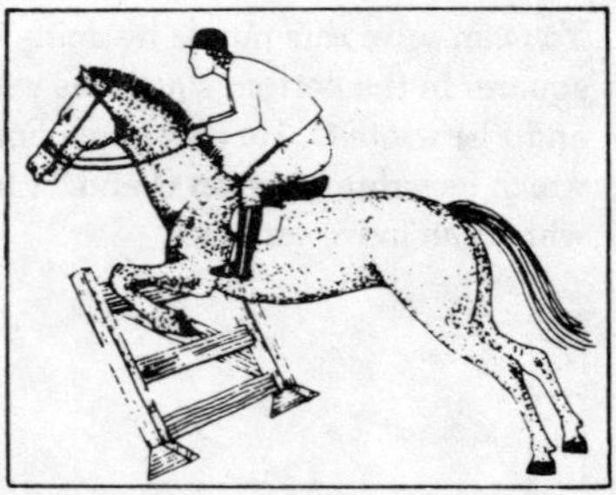

Mr Lake's horse knocked down the first fence.

Four horse-riders (Broom, Hunt, Lake, Mason) entered a jumping competition. There were no other competitors. Mr Broom jumped first. His horse refused to jump the first fence at the first attempt, but jumped it perfectly at the second attempt. He also knocked down the eighth fence. Mr Hunt's horse knocked a pole off the third fence and knocked down the gate at the seventh jump. Mr Lake's horse knocked down the first jump and refused the fourth. He refused to jump it at a second attempt, but went over it perfectly on the third attempt. Mr Mason's horse refused to jump the first fence, but jumped it at the second attempt. He did the same at the second jump, but made no more faults.

Knocking down part of a jump is four faults, and refusing to jump is three faults.

1 Which of the riders had fewest faults and won the competition? ....

2 Who had most faults? ....

25

If Mary gives John one of her sweets, he will have as many as she then has. If, however, John gives Mary one of his sweets, she will have twice as many as he then has. Neither child has more than seven sweets.

How many sweets has John? ....

26

Can you fit these words into the puzzle? Each word describes water in a different form.

ice	rain	puddle	sea	cloud
dew	snow	river	hail	steam

1 When water falls from the clouds it is called . . . .

2 When it freezes and becomes solid, it is called . . . .

3 When a very large amount becomes salty, it is called the . . . .

4 When it fills a hole in the road, it is called a . . . .

5 When it falls from the clouds in white flakes, it is called . . . .

6 When it flows across land, it is called a . . . .

7 When it rises from boiling water, it is called . . . .

8 When it becomes shining drops on grass, it is called . . . .

9 When it falls from the clouds in hard little balls, it is called . . . .

10 When it floats in the sky, it is called a . . . .

27

A bar of chocolate is sometimes divided into six pieces. You can see this in the picture.

Tommy had five bars, and each was divided in this way. Fred, Bobby and Will, his friends, wanted him to share the chocolate equally with them. But Tommy decided to share it according to the number of letters in their names. He therefore gave each boy one piece for each letter of his name.

How many pieces did Tommy keep for himself? . . . .

28

Can you solve this puzzle by finding the missing prepositions? Choose them from the list.

under
against
above
across
through
beside
behind
under

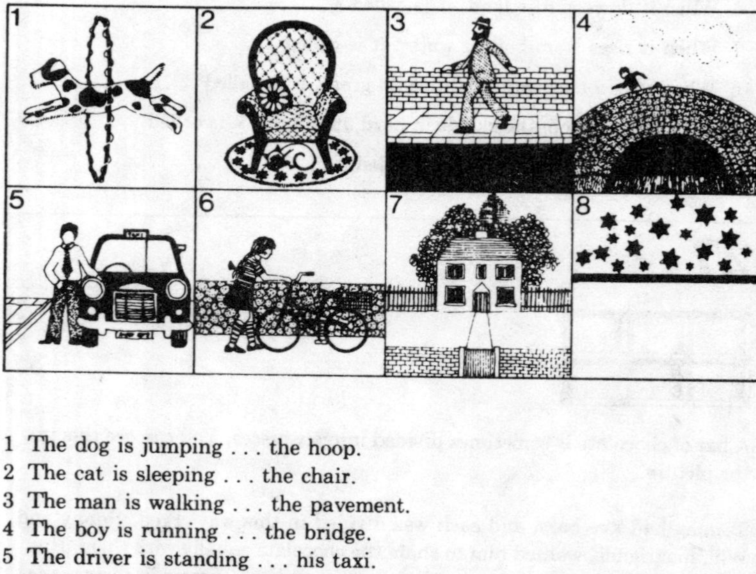

1 The dog is jumping . . . the hoop.
2 The cat is sleeping . . . the chair.
3 The man is walking . . . the pavement.
4 The boy is running . . . the bridge.
5 The driver is standing . . . his taxi.
6 The girl has leant her bicycle . . . the wall.
7 There are some trees . . . the house.
8 There is nothing below the line, but there are some stars . . . it.

29

If you do this puzzle correctly, you will need all these words. Use only one word in each sentence.

weak	correct	nasty	tiny	dangerous
funny	difficult	fair	huge	expensive

1 A .... job is one that you do not like.

2. A .... person has little strength.

3. .... hair is light in colour.

4. A .... answer contains no mistakes.

5. A .... puzzle is not easy; it is hard.

6. A .... bird is very small.

7. .... stories amuse us.

8. An .... dress is dear; you pay a lot for it.

9. A .... building is a very large one.

10. .... driving causes accidents on the road.

30

1 Think of a number. Multiply it by 3. Add 6 to the answer. Divide the result by 3. Take 2 from the answer.

Is the result the same number that you began with? ....

2 Try another number.

Is the last number the same number that you began with again? ....

$9 \times 3 = 27 + 6 = 33 \div 3 = 11 - 2 = 9$
$52 \times 3 = 156 + 6 = 162 \div 3 = 54 - 2 = 52$

31

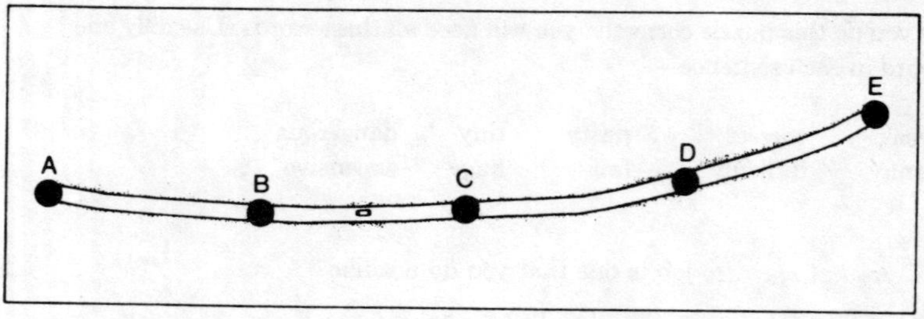

Mr Blake drove from A to E yesterday. He left A at 9.15 in the morning. He reached B 20 minutes later. The journey from B to C took him a half an hour. There were a lot of cars on the road between C and D, and Mr Blake also had to pass through two busy towns. This part of the journey took him three quarters of an hour. He did the last part of his journey in 25 minutes.

1 At what time did he reach E? ....

2 How long did the journey take? ....

32

If you solve this puzzle correctly, the second column down will give you a present participle of a verb. Check your spelling with this list:

snail again light night thing string sting

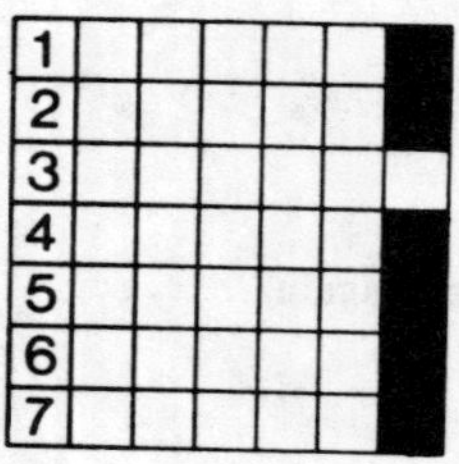

1 An object.
2 The opposite of *heavy*.
3 You tie up parcels with this.
4 Wasps and bees do this.
5 It comes after day time.
6 A soft animal with a shell.
7 Once more.

33

If you solve this puzzle correctly, the first column down will spell a word that means 'not as tall as any of the others'. You have to find the opposites of the clue words.

The opposite of:

1 Fast
2 Cold
3 Young
4 Poor
5 Thick
6 Late
7 Tall
8 False

34

1 Mr Hunt has as many cows on his farm as Mr Wood has; they have the same number. Mr Wood has three cows more than Mr Forest has on his. Mr Hill hasn't as many cows as Mr Forest.

Which of the four farmers has the fewest cows? . . . .

2 Bob has scored the same number of goals as Richard so far this season. He has scored more goals than John, and more than Kevin. Richard has scored fewer goals than Simon.

Which of the five players has scored the most goals? . . . .

35

Can you find these words with the double letters?

1			B	B		
2			D	D		
3			G	G		
4			L	L		
5			M	M		
6			N	N		
7			P	P		
8			S	S		
9			T	T		
10			Z	Z		

1 You rub out with it.
2 You reach high things with it.
3 Larger.
4 The past tense of *fill*.
5 The hottest season.
6 A person who runs.
7 A small meal at night.
8 The past tense of *kiss*.
9 You boil water in it.
10 This is one.

36

1 When Mr Taylor died he left £1,000 to his sons. He had three sons. Martin was 28 years old, James was 25, and the youngest, Peter, was only 20. Mr Brown divided the money in a special way. Each son received £10 for every year of his life and a third of the remainder.

How much did each son receive? ....

....

2 Yesterday Mr Roberts bought a pen, a pencil and a ruler. They cost 40 pence all together. The pencil cost half as much as the ruler, and the pen cost five times as much as the pencil.

How much did each of the three things cost? ....

....

37

Can you find a common English surname? If you fill in correctly the names of the things in the pictures, the first column down will give you the surname.

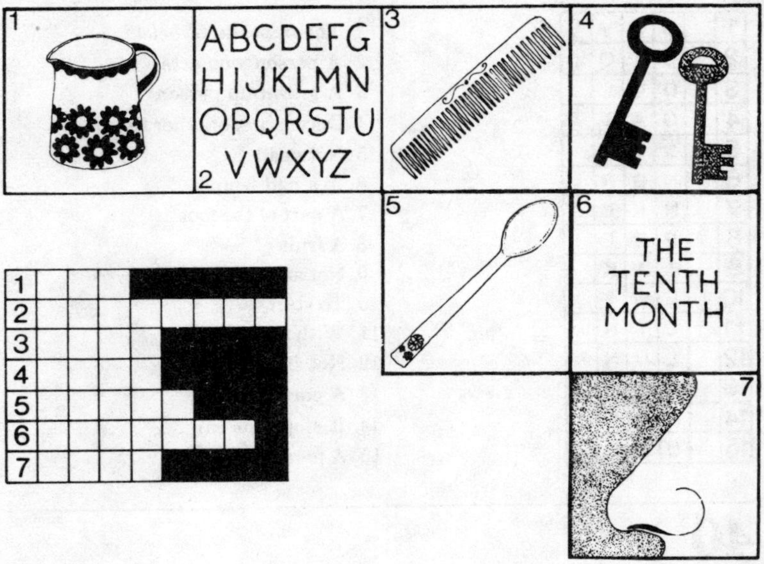

38

It is 3rd April today. Miss Lake's birthday was the day before yesterday, and Miss Brown's was a week before that. The day before her birthday, Miss Lake played tennis. Miss Brown did not play tennis on that day, but she played on the day after her birthday.

1 When was Miss Lake's birthday? ....

2 When was Miss Brown's? ....

3 When did Miss Lake play tennis? ....

4 On what date did Miss Brown play? ....

39

Complete these words by finding the first and last letter of each word.

1		B	O	V	
2		C	T	O	
3		D	U	L	
4		G	A	I	
5		L	I	V	
6		N	G	R	
7		N	K	L	
8		P	P	L	
9		W	A	K	
10		E	G	I	
11		L	I	N	
12		L	U	N	
13		O	U	G	
14		R	A	K	
15		U	Y	E	

1 The opposite of *below*
2 A person who acts
3 A grown-up person
4 Once more; another time
5 Not dead
6 In a bad temper
7 A part of the foot
8 A fruit
9 Not asleep
10 To start
11 With no eye-sight
12 Not sharp
13 A part of a tree
14 It stops the car.
15 A person who buys

40

'There are eight people in this room,' Mr Hall said to his little boy David. 'No one has bad eyes; everyone can see quite well. I am going to put this book somewhere, and one person will not be able to see it, but all the other seven people will be able to see it. Where am I going to put it?'

Where was Mr Hall going to put the book? . . . .

41

The prefix *un-* usually means *not*. You can often make the opposite of an adjective by using this prefix. For example, *uncommon* is the opposite of *common*, and *uncomfortable* is the opposite of *comfortable*.

In this puzzle you have to find eight adjectives that begin with *un-* that will describe the people in the clues. Choose from this list:

unhappy	unlucky	uncertain	unusual
unkind	unwilling	unpopular	unfair

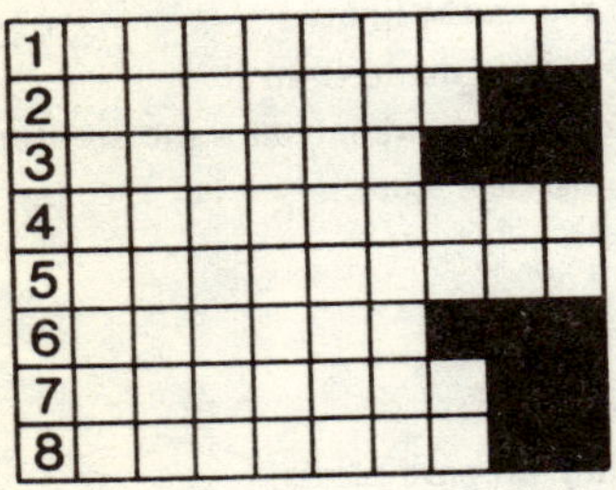

This kind of person

1 is not liked.

2 is sad.

3 is cruel or shows no love.

4 is not sure.

5 does not want to do it.

6 breaks the rules.

7 is not common.

8 does not have any luck.

42

Michael ran round this track seven times. The first time it took him five minutes. But each time he went round he was 30 seconds slower than the time before.

How long did it take him the last time? ....

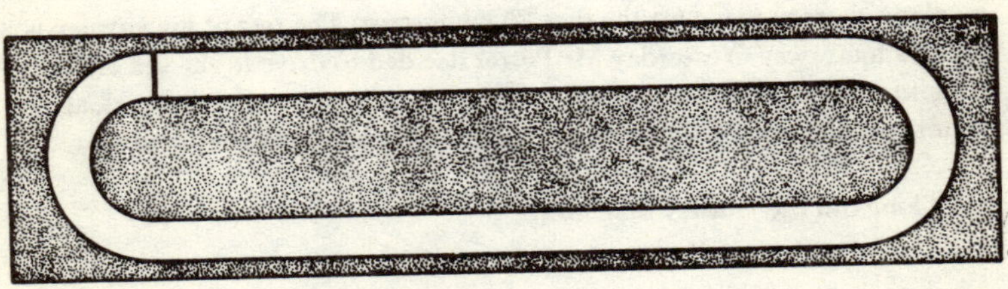

43

The words read down, like this ↘ and up, like this ↗

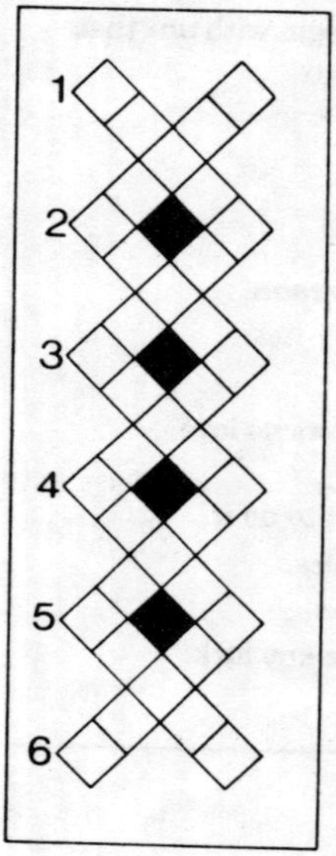

Down

1 It is worn by men, and it hangs from the shoulders.

2 A person does this at the end of the performance of a play, for example.

3 A motorist does this when he comes to red traffic lights.

4 Butter is made from it.

5 You do this when you want to enter someone's room.

Up

2 A boy or a girl.

3 To begin.

4 They prepare meals.

5 The joints between the top and bottom parts of the legs.

6 You sweep the floor with it.

44

Mr Potter lives 40 kilometres from the sea. When he drives there he has to go along country roads for the first 20 kilometres. The rest of his journey is along a motorway. Yesterday Mr Potter decided to drive to the sea and have a swim. He drove at an average speed of 50 kilometres per hour along the country roads and at an average speed of 80 kph along the motorway.

How long did the journey take him? ....

45

The second letter of these 6-letter words is always L. Can you find all 12?

1	L				
2	L				
3	L				
4	L				
5	L				
6	L				
7	L				
8	L				
9	L				
10	L				
11	L				
12	L				

1 At all times.
2 One more than ten.
3 Nearly.
4 A customer.
5 Shut; not open.
6 A kind of shirt for girls.
7 More than one; not singular.
8 Brave.
9 Tired; wanting to sleep.
10 A journey by air.
11 Heavy and ungraceful in movement.
12 The part of a plant that produces seeds.

46

1 Mr Rogers is now three times as old as his son Colin. Seven years ago he was five times as old as Colin.

How old is Colin now? ....

2 'I have some cards in my hand,' said Mrs Stone to her young daughter, Susan. 'If you give me 15 more, I shall have four times as many. How many cards, therefore, have I in my hand?'

How many cards did Mrs Stone have? ....

47

Do you know what rhymes are? The word *tries* rhymes with *flies*, and the word *peas* rhymes with *trees*. Can you find in this list the rhyme words to fit the clues?

ache	trees	high	fork
plate	May	bough	beer

1 It is the opposite of *low* and rhymes with *buy*. 1 ....

2 You eat from it and it rhymes with *eight*. 2 ....

3 It's a part of a tree and rhymes with *cow*. 3 ....

4 It's a month and rhymes with *weigh*. 4 ....

5 They are tall plants and rhyme with *please*. 5 ....

6 You eat with it and it rhymes with *chalk*. 6 ....

7 You drink it and it rhymes with *dear*. 7 ....

8 It's a pain that rhymes with *break*. 8 ....

48

Can you find these rhymes without a check list?

1 It's half of eight and rhymes with *poor*.
2 The opposite of *high* that rhymes with *so*.
3 Small animals that rhyme with *rice*.
4 A part of your head that rhymes with *case*.
5 Twice four that rhymes with *hate*.
6 The colour of the sky that rhymes with *do*.
7 Green vegetables that rhyme with *cheese*.
8 It means in that place and rhymes with *hair*.

49

Words that are often used together are called collocations. *Boys and girls* is a collocation, and *table and chairs* is another. Can you complete the collocations below? Choose the missing words from this list:

forks	children	coat	bacon	saucer	day
paper	country	socks	dogs	poor	bolts
butter	water	ends	tie	nails	pepper

1 bread and . . . .

2 hat and . . . .

3 egg and . . . .

4 knives and . . . .

5 women and . . . .

6 salt and . . . .

7 shoes and . . . .

8 pen and . . . .

9 collar and . . . .

10 soap and . . . .

11 cup and . . . .

12 night and . . . .

13 town and . . . .

14 hammer and . . . .

15 the rich and the . . . .

16 nuts and . . . .

17 cats and . . . .

18 odds and . . . .

50

Mrs Morgan went shopping yesterday. She wanted to buy some oranges, peaches and grapefruit. A peach cost twice as much as an orange, and the price of a grapefruit equalled the price of a peach and an orange together. An orange, a peach and a grapefruit together cost 18 pence. Mrs Morgan decided to buy three oranges, six peaches and five grapefruit.

How much did she pay for them all together? . . . .

grapefruit peach orange

51

1 A train left London for Leeds at 11.15 in the morning. Another train left Leeds for London at the same time. The train from London travelled at 80 kilometres per hour, and the train from Leeds travelled at 100 k.p.h. The distance between the two cities is 300 kilometres. Which train was nearer London when the one passed the other?

. . . .

2 Two groups of hikers were walking along a country road. In the first group there were two girls behind one girl. There was also one girl behind two girls, and there was one girl in the middle. In the other group there was one boy in front of two boys. There were also two boys in front of one boy, and there was a boy in the middle.

How many hikers were there all together? . . . .

3 There were some ostriches and some giraffes behind a high fence. Tommy was not tall enough to see over the fence; he had to look under the fence. He counted 36 legs. There were 11 animals behind the fence. How many were giraffes, and how many were ostriches?

. . . .

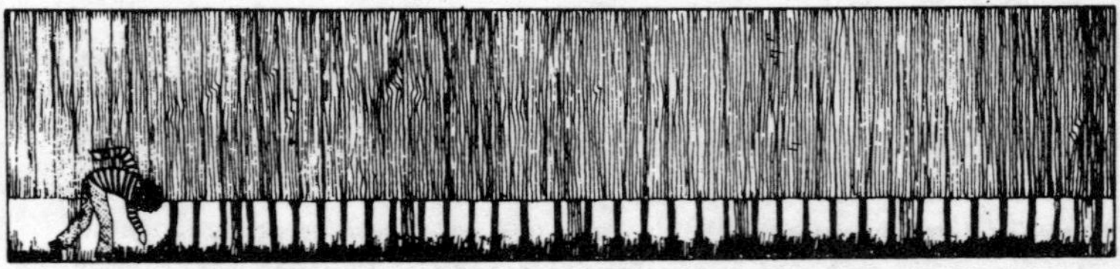

52

Here is the last puzzle. Can you solve it?

1	S				
2		S			
3			S		
4				S	
5					S

1 It is this when the sun shines.
2 Normal; common.
3 Covered with dust.
4 Less than all the others.
5 Bottles are made of this.

Answers

1 1 between 2 Miss Small 3 left 4 ladies 5 Mr Wills 6 right 7 man 8 two

2 1 paints 2 saws 3 cries 4 flies 5 digs 6 shoot 7 sews 8 write 9 drill 10 kicks 11 jump 12 preach 13 learn 14 operate 15 shampoo

3 1 It's a bed. 2 An umbrella does.

4 1 shaving 2 dancing 3 singing 4 laughing 5 digging 6 jumping 7 swimming 8 running 9 smiling 10 riding 11 hitting 12 diving

5 1 bricks 2 cotton 3 paper 4 rubber 5 glass 6 flour 7 steel 8 wood 9 wool 10 grass 11 leather 12 sugar

6 1 Mr White is. 2 She has 25.

7 *North side*: Grey, Pink, Brown, White
South side: Cook, Baker, Butcher, Miller

8 Mr Cook will be.

9 1 tree 2 leg 3 house 4 ship 5 arm 6 foot 7 book 8 shirt 9 bird 10 knife 11 flower 12 car

10 1 Karen is. 2 He had 50p.

11 1 grocer 2 porter 3 jockey 4 chemist 5 sailor 6 artist 7 butcher 8 joiner 9 nurse 10 dentist

12 1 tennis 2 cards 3 bicycle 4 pony 5 hedge 6 lawn 7 pears 8 apples 9 walk

13 1 mother 2 brother 3 kitten 4 under 5 house 6 mouse 7 cheap 8 butter 9 dearer 10 uncle

14 The black one is.

15 1 little 2 dark 3 happy 4 wet 5 asleep 6 wide 7 weak 8 most 9 well 10 closed

16 1 No, it didn't. 2 Carole did.

17 1 sixth 2 usual 3 basin 4 chest 5 class 6 chase 7 dusty 8 Asian 9 scrub

18 1 It's the sun. 2 It's an armchair.

19 1 green 3 child 5 hello 7 early 9 money
2 plate 4 trade 6 large 8 baker

20 1 dirty 3 wrong 5 deep 7 absent 9 narrow
2 easy 4 light 6 alive 8 female 10 quick

21 1 needle 3 saucer 5 brooms 7 cement 9 glasses
2 hammer 4 knives 6 tractor 8 pencils 10 scales

22 ostrich

23 1 start 3 tart 5 smart 7 depart
2 part 4 cart 6 dart 8 heart

24 1 Mr Mason did. 2. Mr Lake did.

25 John has four sweets.

26 1 rain 3 sea 5 snow 7 steam 9 hail
2 ice 4 puddle 6 river 8 dew 10 cloud

27 He kept 17 pieces.

28 1 through 3 along 5 beside 7 behind
2 under 4 across 6 against 8 above

29 1 nasty 3 fair 5 difficult 7 funny 9 huge
2 weak 4 correct 6 tiny 8 expensive 10 dangerous

30 Yes, it is. 2 Yes, it is.

31 1 He reached E at 11.15. 2 It took two hours.

32 1 thing 2 light 3 string 4 sting 5 night 6 snail 7 again

33 1 slow 3 old 5 thin 7 short
2 hot 4 rich 6 early 8 true

34 1 Mr Hill has. 2 Simon has.

35 1 rubber 3 bigger 5 summer 7 supper 9 kettle
2 ladder 4 filled 6 runner 8 kissed 10 puzzle

36 1 Martin received £370, James £340 and Peter £290.
2 The pencil cost 5p, the ruler 10p and the pen 25p.

37 1 jug 3 comb 5 spoon 7 nose
2 alphabet 4 keys 6 October

38 1 It was on 1st April. 3. She played on 31st March.
2 It was on 25th March. 4. She played on 26th March.